How To Find
Gift For Your Loved One

MW00879413

HTeBooks

Disclaimer

This book is designed to provide condensed information. It is not intended to reprint all th information that is otherwise available, but instead to complement, amplify and supplement other texts. You are urged to read all the available material, learn as much as possible and tailor the information to your individual needs.

Every effort has been made to make this book as complete and as accurate as possible. However, ther may be mistakes, both typographical and in content. Therefore, this text should be used only as a general guide and not as the ultimate source of information. The purpose of this book is to educate.

The author or the publisher shall have neither liability nor responsibility to any person or entity with respect to any loss or damage caused, or alleged to have been caused, directly or indirectly, by the information contained in this book.

Table of Contents

How Will This Book Help You?

Have you ever found yourself spending the whole day trying just to get that perfect gift for your loved one? You will agree with me that no matter the amount of cash you are willing to spend on the gift, it ends up being a stressful event. Thankfully, this book is designed to equip you with an understanding of the tricks you can use to ensure your loved one gets a gift that is unique, meaningful and one that brings out their personality. Well, I bet that after reading this book, choosing gifts for your loved one will turn out to be a cherished hobby.

Let this book be a gift to you and use it as the ultimate guide to finding the Perfect Gift for your loved one. Read on...

What Is In A Gift?

"Every gift which is given, even though is be small, is in reality great, if it is given with affection"

- Pindar

The act of giving gifts recurs throughout your life i.e. from th flower you gave to your best friend in first grade to the recent tedd bear you gave your small sister on her birthday. The best thin about receiving gifts is that you don't have to give anything i return.

We associate gifts to occasions whereby we have formed the belie that when it is Christmas, Valentine, or the birth of a new baby, w buy our loved ones gifts. And as it is known, different culture present their gifts in a unique manner. In western culture, a gift ha to be accompanied in a wrapped glittery paper plus a written note indicating the sender whereas the Chinese believe that specifically a red wrapping is symbol for best luck to the person receiving the gift.

While giving gifts during certain occasions is the norm, you should not limit yourself to the normal occasions to present a gift to someone. The best gifts are those, which come randomly and get to surprise the receiver. Use gifts when you want to express your love, show gratitude and as a souvenir.

You should be curious on the types and gift ideas that are available for your loved one. We will be discussing that in the next section so that you can have some ideas on the kind of gifts to buy:

Common Gift Types

It is important for us to look at common ideas of gifts that are given out on many occasions.

Flowers

These are given mostly to ladies who end up displaying the flowers in a vase with some water to keep the flowers fresh. Flowers connote different meanings; for instance, a rose flower shows love.

Artwork

Many people prefer giving out artistic paintings and drawings that bring out the situation at hand. For instance when someone has moved in a new house, a wall hanging of a beautiful house surrounded by a nice garden will fill the house with warmth.

Musical instruments

Playing or listening to music is a cool way of relaxing. At times, giving of music CDs of ones favorite songs, guitar, piano, or a violin is the perfect gift, as your loved one will use it to entertain themselves when bored or going through difficult situations. Furthermore, the gift becomes more practical especially if the receiver plays the specific music instrument you bought them.

Accessories

These come in a wide range, for instance hand watches, necklaces, bracelets, earrings and so on. Since both genders are ardent lovers of these, when buying one, take into consideration, the color and message engraved on them.

Cards

Gift cards have been there for quite a long time. They are used as a gift or supplement of a gift because they contain sweet messages that go hand in hand with an occasion. Although people use them less often in this century, they remain to be significant during special occasions.

Clothing

Being able to choose a cloth or shoe for someone can be very toug because they come in different size and shapes. The best way to gif your loved one with a nice dress, tuxedo or wedge, is to get them gift voucher to their favorite store and even accompany them on th day of buying their preferred clothing.

Books

The advantage with books is that they come in different varieties there are those which are inspirational, religious, for recipes, novels science fiction, comics and the list goes on. If you know the genre that your loved one likes to read, you will find it easy buying them book as a gift as you will not go wrong.

Trips and events

For those who love travelling, a bus ticket to an area that they have never been to sounds exciting. Gifts like trips are those that are stored in your loved ones memory for a long time. Sports events are also enjoyable. For instance, people sell their properties just to attend the world cup match. If your loved one is such a fan, you can make the dream of being present in a world cup match possible if circumstances allow.

In and outdoor games

A set of chess or scrabble games wouldn't hurt for a loved one who has a keen interest in playing such games. These usually appeal to children and teenagers. Toy cars, play stations also can be great gifts. When it comes to outdoor games, a bicycle or a pair of skates is suitable.

While we have looked at common types of gifts that you can give out, it is essential to have some important factors in mind when buying a gift in order to get a suitable gift for whoever you are buying the gift for. Actually, these factors are what you should have in mind when buying gifts. In the next chapter, we shall look at the

ctors you should put in mind before buying a gift for your loved
ne.

Key point/action step

There is no limit to the type of gift that you can buy provided that
the gift that you buy is functional to the person receiving. In any
case, as we have seen in this chapter, it is not just about the gift that
you give (though giving a good gift is important) but rather, it is the
thought that counts.

Why Give Gifts

"From what we get, we can make a living; what we give, howeve: makes a life."

- Arthur Ashe

In order for you to go out of your way and just get the perfect gif you will need to understand the importance of giving gifts. This helpful so that the next time you are getting your friend a brida shower, or a birthday gift, you don't feel as if looking for a gift is chore but rather something that you want to do for your loved one.

Cultural demands

The act of giving gifts started a long time ago and has been embedded in our traditions. We make a point of giving gifts on special occasions like Christmas, New Year, anniversaries and so on This enables you to mark those special events in your life and our need to continue giving is in practice of keeping the tradition of giving alive.

To show affection

Our loved ones are of great value to us. It therefore becomes significant to strengthen the bonds between us by giving them gifts every once in a while. You should practice this more often as it may communicate your feelings of love, care and support to your loved ones much better than words would. In so doing you will maintain a healthy relationship with all your loved ones. For instance in a case where the wife is showered with gifts by the husband, you find the house to be peaceful and everything runs smoothly.

Token of appreciation

In life, we go through so many ups and downs, which dampen our hopes for the future. In most cases, our loved ones are always there to hold our hands hence they end up helping in carrying the burdens. What best way to show them our gratitude other than buying them gifts that they will treasure? This will make them feel appreciated for the support they gave us.

Exercise your skills

Gifts come in different forms. When you have a talent in a field such as art and craft, music and playing instruments, you should use it by giving them as either a product or service to your loved one. For instance, making a bracelet using beads and giving it as a gift to your loved one will show that you took your time and effort for that person. Singing to your loved one is also a gift that will make them appreciate who you are and the skills you possess.

Achievements

We use gifts to reward efforts made by our loved ones, for instance when they have performed well at work or in school. This creates a sense of motivation in our loved ones as the gift makes them more active and they strive to do more and achieve better results in the days to come.

Time

We have discussed on importance of giving gifts. However much the positivity portrayed after the act is performed, you should remember that giving your time is the most important gift that you can give to your loved ones. Irrespective of the size or price of the gift you shower your loved ones with, when you never seem to spend time with your loved ones then they will never find the happiness that they deserve. Your loved ones need to be shown love and affection more by your presence and this is also how you will get to know their likes and dislikes which you will use in the long run when choosing a gift that defines them best.

All of the above actions when coupled up with time will make your life enjoyable. Remember too that a perfect gift is one, which is given purely from the heart with no expected gains. This is the only way your loved ones won't feel pressure of living up to some expectations.

*Key point/action step

Giving gifts is an old tradition that is not going anywhere. While our goal is to get the perfect gift for our loved ones, remember that you can only get that great gift only if you know how important giving gifts is. Once you realize this, then you will not take the act of giving gifts as some sort of chore that you need to do. This change of attitude is what will make you go out of your way just to get that perfect gift.

What To Consider Before Buying A Gift

"Giving presents is a talent; to know what a person wants, to know when and how to get it, to give it lovingly and well. Unless character possesses this talent there is no moment more annihilating to ease than that in which a present is received and given."

- Pamela Glenconner

When you want to give a gift, what's the first thing that comes to your mind? Even if giving a gift is an emotional affair, you don't want to end up giving the wrong kind of gifts to your loved ones. As such, you need some sort of blueprint to help you settle on a nice gift. Here are some of the factors to consider;

Relationship you have with the recipient of gift

You may want to give a gift to your sister, wife, husband, mother, or father. What matters in terms of the gift you will choose for either of them will depend with the closeness that you have with them. Your relationship level is important, as there are some gifts you cannot present to your parents or your siblings. For instance, if it is your wife, buying a gift like lingerie will not be a problem because you have intimate relationship whereas you can buy a briefcase for your father, which will not be appropriate for your sister.

Occasion

We buy different gifts depending on the occasion. Common occasions include birthdays, Christmas, Valentine and New Year. As tradition puts it, it becomes difficult to separate ourselves from those occasions. Having this in mind when you want to give a gift will ensure that you buy the appropriate one. For instance, on alentine's Day, the presents are mostly those that portray your elings of love to your partner such as flowers and I love you cards; us, matching a gift with the right message for the occasion is ideal.

Your Budget

his is crucial in everything you do. When buying a gift for your oved one I am sure you would want to get the best, which in most ases means spending more money. You should make a point of reating a budget for the gift you want to buy or make for your loved ne. It is quite evident that there is a certain amount you are willing o spend. Your loved one may be one who prefers handmade gifts ather than those bought in shops whereas there are people who issociate a good gift as one that you have invested a lot of money. Having the right budget will help you in choosing the right gift and woiding overspending which usually is a strain on your part.

Age

It comes as a defining factor since some presents cannot apply to an idult as well as a child. How will it an elderly man take it if you presented him with a gift of a ticket to a rock band concert? Well, much as people are different, most elderly people may take it as a big joke and a sign of disrespect. Such a gift would have been more suitable to a teenager or young adult. Also, don't gift an adult a kid's toy especially if they don't have kids.

Gender

Men and women are very different in nature. From the shoes they wear to the accessories; I am sure we are all aware of this. Some things that fascinate men rarely have a positive response from women. Buying gifts for women is seen to be a complex ordeal than shopping for men. This is because women are more emotional and put their feelings into the products or services that they receive. For instance, while men are more attracted to gifts like electronics and sportswear, women prefer flowers, jewelry and cosmetics.

Hobby and Interest

Think about how your loved one spends their time, what they like talking about and what they treasure around in the house. Is your loved one a sports fan, student or chef? This will help you narrow down the kind of gift you choose for them. When he or she talks, be careful enough to listen to what they wish for, take note if possible and make an effort of surprising them with the particular gift. A ticket to a football match if they are sports fan will surely excite them.

Occupation

A farmer may prefer a new hoe, journalist a camera and musician a guitar etc. Taking into consideration the job that your loved one does will be a good guide in helping you get them the perfect gift. It is wise also as the gift will be put into use so long as the person remains in that job. Nevertheless, before buying that guitar or the other gifts, it's advisable to find out the certain type that works best with their jobs so as to avoid disappointing the recipient and yourself when your gift is not functional.

Personality

Your personality makes you choosy when it comes to colors, dressing, accessories and the type of reading materials you prefer. Actually, some people still prefer the traditional way of doing things than the 'digitalized' modern ways. For instance, while some people love the new and trendy phones available, there are those who prefer the old-fashioned kind of phones. Thus, you may end up having to buy what you consider old fashioned in order for the gift to achieve its intended purpose.

ow that you have taken the necessary considerations outlined bove, what next? It's time to get into the core of the matter which to know the tips and tricks to get the perfect gift.

Key point/action step

utting into consideration the factors outlined in this chapter is nportant, as it will ensure that you choose the perfect gift that will e functional. You would not want a situation whereby you buy a articular gift thinking that it is perfect only for the recipient to hink otherwise.

Tips And Tricks Of Finding The Perfec Gift

"To give anything less than your best, is to sacrifice the gift."
- Steve Prefontaine

Gift giving can make us resentful when it feels like a chore. We a times give gifts so as to get something in return such as gratitud from the person receiving it. Before gifting anything, you have t detach yourself from it such that you don't expect anything from th recipient.

In many instances, when you want to choose a perfect gift for you loved one, you find yourself doing multiple calculations in you head, What do they want? What do they need? Where can I find it How will I present it? All these questions pop in your mind yet you had been planning to buy the gift for some time now. What it shows is that you had not prepared well enough on a gift that will please your loved one.

In this chapter, we are going to tackle the tips you should follow before and after buying a gift so as to keep you prepared at all times;

Research

You already know that before giving a gift you should consider your loved one's taste, interests, and preferences. A trick of doing so is doing a thorough research on the person receiving the gift to find out what they like, their interests and even hobbies. Apart from the obvious things, you know about them, you will be surprised about the inward interests that they don't share with you. Use your loved one's social media accounts to identify this. If it means going to their best friends to get their angle on your loved one's interest, then do it. Research should not be limited to your loved one but also to the different gift ideas and the places to buy them. A great place o look for suitable gifts is on online stores like etsy, ebay and mazon. You are sure to find amazing out of this world gifts.

Make a list

A list makes a person organized and be able to do things efficiently. The best gift is one, which reflects personality and interests of someone. A list therefore gives you an opportunity of brainstorming on your loved one's hobbies, skills and likes. In so doing, you will come up with a long-list of gifts but this does not necessarily mean that you will buy all these gifts. Narrow it down to the most essential that you presume will catch the attention of your wife, husband, son, friend or daughter; basically, whoever you will be giving the gift.

Do It Yourself

This is the best place to get your creative juices flowing with all the amazing ideas available. Let's be real, it can really be expensive to buy gifts during holidays, New Year's Eve and Valentine to add on Weddings and Birthdays. Luckily, you can make gifts that are touching and impressive with little time and effort. I believe that we all have our creative side that we can tap into. Additionally, the recipient is even more likely to love a DIY gift than something that you just bought at the dollar store or at a high-end boutique. Let us have a look at amazing inexpensive gift ideas that you can try:

Animated Key Chains

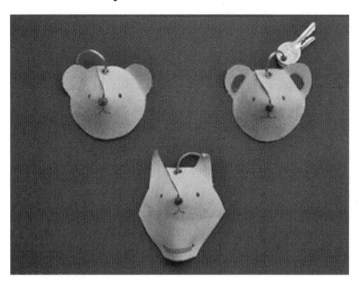

Cookies in a jar

emstone Jar

Rose Petals in jar

Surprise

No one likes an obvious gift or one they can buy themselves. As much as you should listen to your loved one's hints of gifts they want, it will be more exciting and fulfilling to your loved one when you surprise them with something that they liked but dreamt of it as impossibility. Giving a surprise gift makes it more appealing. For instance, pretend in the morning that you have forgotten that day is your second anniversary then when you come in the evening after work, tell your wife that you want to take them for a romantic dinner out of town to celebrate the years you have been together.

Do charity in their name

There are so many organizations that stand for a nobble cause such as orphanages, institutes of patients with HIV/AIDS or cancer. At times, indirect gifting goes a long way than giving a gift directly. If your loved one is a member of an organization that stands for a certain cause or is a charitable person all year round, you can give them the gift of giving things like money or foodstuffs to a children's home in their name. This will be a perfect gift on their end.

A gift of labor

You can look around the house of the person you want to buy a gift to determine if there is something physically that needs to be done which you are capable of. An example is changing of lighting bulbs, using a fresh coat of paint on the walls and repairing a broken cabinet. Use your energy to help in renovating the house hence increasing the value of their home. This will make the rooms appear new and relaxing and they will always remember what you did as long as the work is there, what a perfect gift!

Have you narrowed down your search for a perfect gift? This helpful information will make sense when coupled up with how, when and where you should give the gift discussed. This is discussed in the next chapter.

Key point/action step

gift that has not been well thought is not a gift worth giving. If you re not sure if you are getting the right gift, it is much better to wait. s we have seen in this chapter, if you are creative, you can make ome amazing DIY gifts that will amaze your loved ones. However, you don't have the time to come up with a suitable gift, the best ption would be to buy the gift from such sites like etsy that sell andcrafted and unique items.

How, Where And When To Give Gifts To A Loved One

"Every gift is held by two hands: the one that gives, and the one that takes away."

- Tony D'Souza, Whiteman

You are excited as you've already chosen a gift that you deem perfect for your loved one but not all covered as the challenge of presenting it to them still lies on your shoulder. The defining moment is how and when is the best way to present the gift to avoid pitfalls. This chapter will give you an insight on how you will go about presenting your gift and at the same time ensuring it remains perfect.

Wrap the gift

Before you can even think of how and where you will give the gift, you need to wrap it first. Be very keen and considerate about this, as it can make or break your presentation of the gift. Use a wrapping paper and a box to wrap it nicely so that you don't make it obvious based on the shape or size. Depending on how you wrap the gift, it can show some respect and sense of style. A wrapped gift also portrays the care of presenting the gift nicely. A wrapped gift also makes the recipient eager to know the present that is inside making their faces lighten up when opening the wrapped gift and definitely this will give you great joy.

Venue

So, where is the best place to give out a gift? I can't really say that there are specific locations that you should or should not give a gift. However, the venue that you should choose when you want to

esent the gift should have some qualities. One of them is a cool
niet place; it is not right to give a gift in a noisy place where there
a lot of distractions. This is because you want your loved one to
ay attention to what you want to say to them and you also need to
e their expression when opening the gift. In a busy street, market,
shopping mall, they might just put the gift in their bag and forget
open it on the same day when they reach home. Presenting it in a
staurant when having a dinner or at home is good enough.

ituation

ou want your gift to be received warmly and wholeheartedly by
our loved one. You should therefore ensure that your timing of
resenting the gift is suitable. A person's mood usually clouds their
udgment. When you present a gift to your loved one when they are
n a bad mood, mourning or depressed, they will receive it with less
nthusiasm than when they are in a joyful mood. Never also try to
ive a gift when you have wronged someone as a way to apologize so
s to cover up your wrongs. Instead, make the apology first without
gift and ensure you are in good terms when giving the gift.

While we have looked at things to consider when buying a gift as
well as how to present a gift, there are also many mistakes that
people make when buying and presenting gifts. Let's have a look at
these mistakes.

*Key point/action step

However good and amazing a gift is, how it is presented can make
or break the gift in question. Always ensure that you wrap your gift
nicely, choose a suitable place to give the gift and ensure that you
are in good terms with the recipient if you want them to be
enthusiastic about the gift you have for them.

Mistakes To Avoid When Choosing Or Giving Gifts

"Experience is that marvelous thing that enables you to recognize mistake when you make it again. "

- Franklin P. Jones

Show pride in the gift that you want to choose. Do not buy a gift just because you saw it in an advert or a store; instead, put your time and effort while purchasing or personally making the gift. It is definitely disappointing when you find out that the gift you gave a loved one was given to another person as a gift, donated to a charity or thrown away. The only way to ensure that there will be maximum satisfaction to you and your loved one is to avoid these common mistakes that you might be making when choosing gifts.

Shopping for yourself

It is very annoying when you receive a gift that portrays the personality and interests of the giver. People make this mistake consciously or unconsciously. Just because you love a particular color, fashion sense and looks does not mean that your loved one shares the same feelings. To make your gift perfect, get to know the personality of your loved one. This will show you care.

In the same light, avoid generalizations or stereotyping. Not every boy is a football fun and not every girl loves chocolates. There are men who would choose a movie ticket over a football ticket and women who prefer books to flowers.

Buying common gifts

There are gifts that are too common and obvious. For instance, in most cases, during Valentine, most people receive chocolates and owers from their boyfriends, girlfriends, spouses etc. I think ometimes we overdo this. I am not saying that chocolates are bad ut rather buy an out of the ordinary gift like her favorite movie, ecipe book or anything that is out of the ordinary and not the orm. I always insist that you buy something unique and that is ifficult to find in the stores such that the receiver might be curious n how you managed to get them such a gift.

Materialistic in your gifting

We like giving tangible gifts that may not be communicating something to the receiver not realizing that it is not about the gift but what the gift tells the receiver. You would want the gift to be engraved in their memories for years to come. Subjecting them to some experience will be a worthy gift. For instance, making them to participate in daring things like mountain climbing, bungee jumping or skydiving is just but a few ideas.

Last minute rush

We like going to buy gifts on the particular day of the occasion but end up being disappointed; this is a common mistake that we make. When you do not plan and buy a gift in advance, you will get confused moving from one store to another trying to choose a gift and in the end, you may settle for less or something you did not want to buy. The secret is planning early and buying the gift a week before the occasion. For instance during Christmas season, gifts are mostly bought in the stores a day before Christmas.

Non-gifts

Those items in the house, which are a necessity, should not be a gift that you buy for your loved one, especially the ones that will be used by the whole family. This is because a gift is meant to be personal and for a specific person for them to keep as a treasure. For instance, a scrubbing brush, plates or glasses can be used by every family member making it cease to be treasured. If you give you loved one a painting, it is something that won't be available for jus anyone.

*Key point/action step

How can you give an amazing gift when you continue making th same mistakes repeatedly? I hope this book has helped you realiz the many mistakes that people make when buying and presentin; gifts so that you can avoid making the same mistakes. Avoidin; these mistakes will ensure that you have a better gifting experience.

How to Apply What You've Learned?

In conclusion, the act of giving is a true art- we can summarize a the tips that we have learned into three steps. Step one is understand the person whom you intend to give the gift. Afte understanding them, settle down on the gift that they truly wan and work on getting the gift then present the gift to them in a nic way so as to complete the gifting process. Don't be ignorant; follow these guides for a rewarding effect in your gifting. Research ha shown that giving is good for you as it reduces the chances of stres and depression. I would urge that you make it a passion and do i more often, whether there is an occasion or not.

Made in the USA
Columbia, SC
23 December 2024

50494174R00017